THE HORSE TRAVEL JOURNAL

A LOG BOOK FOR LONG RIDERS

EDITED BY

CUCHULLAINE O'REILLY F.R.G.S.

The Long Riders' Guild Press

www.horsetravelbooks.com

ISBN: 978-1-59048-288-9

DEDICATION

THE HORSE TRAVEL JOURNAL IS DEDICATED TO THE MODERN
ROAD HORSE.
WE SET OUT TOGETHER ON A SACRED ADVENTURE,
ENTRUSTING OUR SOULS TO THEIR CARE.
THE SOUND OF THEIR HOOF-BEATS IS OUR ANTHEM.
THE SONG OF ROMANCE IS THE CHORUS WE SING WITH THEM.
OURS IS A SECRET MELODY COMPOSED OF LEAN TIMES AND
HARD MILES.
EVENTUALLY THEY BRING US TO THE EDGE OF EXISTENCE -
TO A SACRED PLACE CALLED ELSEWHERE.

THIS JOURNAL IS THE PROPERTY OF:

Name: _____

Address: _____

_____

_____

Tel: _____

Email: _____

THIS JOURNAL IS OF HISTORICAL AND GEOGRAPHICAL IMPORTANCE. IF THE LONG RIDER CANNOT BE LOCATED, PLEASE SEND IT TO:

THE LONG RIDERS' GUILD
C/O THE MEMBERSHIP MANAGER
ROYAL GEOGRAPHICAL SOCIETY
1 KENSINGTON GORE
LONDON SW7 2AR
GREAT BRITAIN

THIS HORSE TRAVEL JOURNAL INCLUDES NOTES AND OBSERVATIONS WRITTEN BY

_____

DURING A JOURNEY

FROM _____

TO _____

DATE: _____

ALL MATERIAL HELD WITHIN THIS JOURNAL IS THE SOLE INTELLECTUAL PROPERTY OF THE EQUESTRIAN EXPLORER DESIGNATED AS THE OWNER.

TABLE OF CONTENTS

Page

SAMPLE

Date: July 29th 2000
# of days on journey: 34
Journey today from: Warai
Journey today to: Pani Kot
Departure time: 05.45 a.m.
Arrival time: 3.00 p.m.
Distance today: 37 miles
Total distance: 573 miles

Nature of country:
Road: fair condition, leads gradually uphill out of
Warai. Leave desert country halfway to Paki Kot and
enter increasingly rocky terrain. Pass several villages,
people friendly. Cross two bridges, both very bad.
Lowari Pass in sight by 1 p.m.

Weather:
Generally cooler
Temperature: 76 F.   **Altitude:** 7,681 feet.

Condition of Horses:
Horses under saddle nearly ten hours today. Average
speed over bad terrain 3 m.p.h. All horses are hungry.
Poor food for several days now. Pukhtoon's pack
saddle slipped. Pompeii full of life. Still no sign of
Pasha.

Preparation for next day's journey:
See map # 7. Check all horseshoes and equipment
before heading over Lowari Pass tomorrow. In 1926
last mounted British army patrol passed through Pani
Kot.

Notes:

_____
_____
_____
_____
_____
_____
_____
_____
_____
_____
_____
_____
_____
_____
_____
_____
_____
_____
_____
_____
_____
_____
_____
_____
_____
_____
_____
_____
_____
_____

Date: _____

# of days on journey: _____

Journey today from: _____

Journey today to: _____

Departure time: _____

Arrival time: _____

Distance today: _____

Total distance: _____

Nature of country:

_____

_____

_____

_____

Weather:

_____

_____

Temperature: _____   Altitude: _____

Condition of Horses:

_____

_____

_____

_____

_____

_____

_____

_____

Preparation for next day's journey:

_____

_____

_____

_____

Notes:

_____

_____

_____

_____

_____

_____

_____

_____

_____

_____

_____

_____

_____

_____

_____

_____

_____

_____

_____

_____

_____

_____

_____

_____

_____

_____

_____

_____

_____

_____

The Horse Travel Journal

Date: _____

\# of days on journey: _____

Journey today from: _____

Journey today to: _____

Departure time: _____

Arrival time: _____

Distance today: _____

Total distance: _____

Nature of country:

_____

_____

_____

_____

Weather:

_____

_____

Temperature: _____   Altitude: _____

Condition of Horses:

_____

_____

_____

_____

_____

_____

_____

_____

Preparation for next day's journey:

_____

_____

_____

_____

Notes:

_____

_____

_____

_____

_____

_____

_____

_____

_____

_____

_____

_____

_____

_____

_____

_____

_____

_____

_____

_____

_____

_____

_____

_____

_____

_____

_____

_____

Date: _____

# of days on journey: _____

Journey today from: _____

Journey today to: _____

Departure time: _____

Arrival time: _____

Distance today: _____

Total distance: _____

Nature of country:

_____

_____

_____

_____

Weather:

_____

_____

Temperature: _____   Altitude: _____

Condition of Horses:

_____

_____

_____

_____

_____

_____

_____

Preparation for next day's journey:

_____

_____

_____

_____

Notes:

_____

_____

_____

_____

_____

_____

_____

_____

_____

_____

_____

_____

_____

_____

_____

_____

_____

_____

_____

_____

_____

_____

_____

_____

_____

_____

_____

_____

_____

_____

_____

_____

_____

Date: _____

# of days on journey: _____

Journey today from: _____

Journey today to: _____

Departure time: _____

Arrival time: _____

Distance today: _____

Total distance: _____

Nature of country:

_____

_____

_____

_____

Weather:

_____

_____

Temperature: _____   Altitude: _____

Condition of Horses:

_____

_____

_____

_____

_____

_____

_____

_____

Preparation for next day's journey:

_____

_____

_____

_____

Notes:

_____
_____
_____
_____
_____
_____
_____
_____
_____
_____
_____
_____
_____
_____
_____
_____
_____
_____
_____
_____
_____
_____
_____
_____
_____
_____
_____
_____
_____
_____
_____

Date: _____

# of days on journey: _____

Journey today from: _____

Journey today to: _____

Departure time: _____

Arrival time: _____

Distance today: _____

Total distance: _____

Nature of country:

_____

_____

_____

_____

Weather:

_____

_____

Temperature: _____   Altitude: _____

Condition of Horses:

_____

_____

_____

_____

_____

_____

_____

Preparation for next day's journey:

_____

_____

_____

_____

Notes:

_____

_____

_____

_____

_____

_____

_____

_____

_____

_____

_____

_____

_____

_____

_____

_____

_____

_____

_____

_____

_____

_____

_____

_____

_____

_____

_____

_____

_____

_____

_____

_____

Date: _____

# of days on journey: _____

Journey today from: _____

Journey today to: _____

Departure time: _____

Arrival time: _____

Distance today: _____

Total distance: _____

Nature of country:

_____

_____

_____

_____

Weather:

_____

_____

Temperature: _____   Altitude: _____

Condition of Horses:

_____

_____

_____

_____

_____

_____

_____

_____

Preparation for next day's journey:

_____

_____

_____

_____

The Horse Travel Journal

Notes:

_____

_____

_____

_____

_____

_____

_____

_____

_____

_____

_____

_____

_____

_____

_____

_____

_____

_____

_____

_____

_____

_____

_____

_____

_____

_____

_____

_____

_____

_____

_____

_____

Date: _____

# of days on journey: _____

Journey today from: _____

Journey today to: _____

Departure time: _____

Arrival time: _____

Distance today: _____

Total distance: _____

Nature of country:

_____

_____

_____

_____

Weather:

_____

_____

Temperature: _____   Altitude: _____

Condition of Horses:

_____

_____

_____

_____

_____

_____

_____

_____

Preparation for next day's journey:

_____

_____

_____

_____

Notes:

_____

_____

_____

_____

_____

_____

_____

_____

_____

_____

_____

_____

_____

_____

_____

_____

_____

_____

_____

_____

_____

_____

_____

_____

_____

_____

_____

_____

_____

_____

_____

Date: _____

\# of days on journey: _____

Journey today from: _____

Journey today to: _____

Departure time: _____

Arrival time: _____

Distance today: _____

Total distance: _____

Nature of country:

_____

_____

_____

_____

Weather:

_____

_____

Temperature: _____   Altitude: _____

Condition of Horses:

_____

_____

_____

_____

_____

_____

_____

_____

Preparation for next day's journey:

_____

_____

_____

_____

Notes:

_____

_____

_____

_____

_____

_____

_____

_____

_____

_____

_____

_____

_____

_____

_____

_____

_____

_____

_____

_____

_____

_____

_____

_____

_____

_____

_____

_____

Date: _____

\# of days on journey: _____

Journey today from: _____

Journey today to: _____

Departure time: _____

Arrival time: _____

Distance today: _____

Total distance: _____

Nature of country:

_____
_____
_____
_____

Weather:

_____
_____

Temperature: _____   Altitude: _____

Condition of Horses:

_____
_____
_____
_____
_____
_____
_____

Preparation for next day's journey:

_____
_____
_____
_____

Notes:

_____

_____

_____

_____

_____

_____

_____

_____

_____

_____

_____

_____

_____

_____

_____

_____

_____

_____

_____

_____

_____

_____

_____

_____

_____

_____

_____

_____

_____

_____

_____

_____

_____

_____

_____

Date: _____

\# of days on journey: _____

Journey today from: _____

Journey today to: _____

Departure time: _____

Arrival time: _____

Distance today: _____

Total distance: _____

Nature of country:

_____

_____

_____

_____

Weather:

_____

_____

Temperature: _____   Altitude: _____

Condition of Horses:

_____

_____

_____

_____

_____

_____

_____

_____

Preparation for next day's journey:

_____

_____

_____

_____

Notes:

_____

_____

_____

_____

_____

_____

_____

_____

_____

_____

_____

_____

_____

_____

_____

_____

_____

_____

_____

_____

_____

_____

_____

_____

_____

_____

_____

_____

_____

_____

_____

_____

_____

_____

_____

_____

Date: _____

# of days on journey: _____

Journey today from: _____

Journey today to: _____

Departure time: _____

Arrival time: _____

Distance today: _____

Total distance: _____

Nature of country:

_____

_____

_____

_____

Weather:

_____

_____

Temperature: _____   Altitude: _____

Condition of Horses:

_____

_____

_____

_____

_____

_____

_____

Preparation for next day's journey:

_____

_____

_____

_____

Notes:

_____
_____
_____
_____
_____
_____
_____
_____
_____
_____
_____
_____
_____
_____
_____
_____
_____
_____
_____
_____
_____
_____
_____
_____
_____
_____
_____
_____
_____
_____
_____
_____
_____
_____

Date: _____

# of days on journey: _____

Journey today from: _____

Journey today to: _____

Departure time: _____

Arrival time: _____

Distance today: _____

Total distance: _____

Nature of country:

_____

_____

_____

_____

Weather:

_____

_____

Temperature: _____   Altitude: _____

Condition of Horses:

_____

_____

_____

_____

_____

_____

_____

_____

Preparation for next day's journey:

_____

_____

_____

_____

Notes:

_____

_____

_____

_____

_____

_____

_____

_____

_____

_____

_____

_____

_____

_____

_____

_____

_____

_____

_____

_____

_____

_____

_____

_____

_____

_____

_____

_____

Date: _____

# of days on journey: _____

Journey today from: _____

Journey today to: _____

Departure time: _____

Arrival time: _____

Distance today: _____

Total distance: _____

Nature of country:

_____

_____

_____

_____

Weather:

_____

_____

Temperature: _____   Altitude: _____

Condition of Horses:

_____

_____

_____

_____

_____

_____

_____

_____

Preparation for next day's journey:

_____

_____

_____

_____

Notes:

_____
_____
_____
_____
_____
_____
_____
_____
_____
_____
_____
_____
_____
_____
_____
_____
_____
_____
_____
_____
_____
_____
_____
_____
_____
_____
_____
_____
_____
_____
_____
_____
_____

Date: _____

# of days on journey: _____

Journey today from: _____

Journey today to: _____

Departure time: _____

Arrival time: _____

Distance today: _____

Total distance: _____

Nature of country:

_____

_____

_____

_____

Weather:

_____

_____

Temperature: _____   Altitude: _____

Condition of Horses:

_____

_____

_____

_____

_____

_____

_____

Preparation for next day's journey:

_____

_____

_____

_____

The Horse Travel Journal

Notes:

_____
_____
_____
_____
_____
_____
_____
_____
_____
_____
_____
_____
_____
_____
_____
_____
_____
_____
_____
_____
_____
_____
_____
_____
_____
_____
_____
_____
_____
_____
_____

Date: _____

\# of days on journey: _____

Journey today from: _____

Journey today to: _____

Departure time: _____

Arrival time: _____

Distance today: _____

Total distance: _____

Nature of country:

_____

_____

_____

_____

Weather:

_____

_____

Temperature: _____   Altitude: _____

Condition of Horses:

_____

_____

_____

_____

_____

_____

_____

Preparation for next day's journey:

_____

_____

_____

_____

Notes:

_____

_____

_____

_____

_____

_____

_____

_____

_____

_____

_____

_____

_____

_____

_____

_____

_____

_____

_____

_____

_____

_____

_____

_____

_____

_____

_____

_____

_____

_____

_____

_____

_____

Date: _____

\# of days on journey: _____

Journey today from: _____

Journey today to: _____

Departure time: _____

Arrival time: _____

Distance today: _____

Total distance: _____

Nature of country:

_____

_____

_____

_____

Weather:

_____

_____

Temperature: _____   Altitude: _____

Condition of Horses:

_____

_____

_____

_____

_____

_____

_____

_____

Preparation for next day's journey:

_____

_____

_____

_____

Notes:

_____

_____

_____

_____

_____

_____

_____

_____

_____

_____

_____

_____

_____

_____

_____

_____

_____

_____

_____

_____

_____

_____

_____

_____

_____

_____

_____

_____

_____

_____

_____

_____

_____

_____

Date: _____

# of days on journey: _____

Journey today from: _____

Journey today to: _____

Departure time: _____

Arrival time: _____

Distance today: _____

Total distance: _____

Nature of country:

_____

_____

_____

_____

Weather:

_____

_____

Temperature: _____   Altitude: _____

Condition of Horses:

_____

_____

_____

_____

_____

_____

_____

_____

Preparation for next day's journey:

_____

_____

_____

_____

41Notes:

_____

_____

_____

_____

_____

_____

_____

_____

_____

_____

_____

_____

_____

_____

_____

_____

_____

_____

_____

_____

_____

_____

_____

_____

_____

_____

_____

_____

_____

_____

Date: _____

# of days on journey: _____

Journey today from: _____

Journey today to: _____

Departure time: _____

Arrival time: _____

Distance today: _____

Total distance: _____

Nature of country:

_____

_____

_____

_____

Weather:

_____

_____

Temperature: _____   Altitude: _____

Condition of Horses:

_____

_____

_____

_____

_____

_____

_____

_____

Preparation for next day's journey:

_____

_____

_____

_____

Notes:

_____

_____

_____

_____

_____

_____

_____

_____

_____

_____

_____

_____

_____

_____

_____

_____

_____

_____

_____

_____

_____

_____

_____

_____

_____

_____

_____

_____

Date: _____

# of days on journey: _____

Journey today from: _____

Journey today to: _____

Departure time: _____

Arrival time: _____

Distance today: _____

Total distance: _____

Nature of country:

_____

_____

_____

_____

Weather:

_____

_____

Temperature: _____   Altitude: _____

Condition of Horses:

_____

_____

_____

_____

_____

_____

_____

_____

Preparation for next day's journey:

_____

_____

_____

_____

Notes:

Date: _____

# of days on journey: _____

Journey today from: _____

Journey today to: _____

Departure time: _____

Arrival time: _____

Distance today: _____

Total distance: _____

Nature of country:

_____

_____

_____

_____

Weather:

_____

_____

Temperature: _____   Altitude: _____

Condition of Horses:

_____

_____

_____

_____

_____

_____

_____

Preparation for next day's journey:

_____

_____

_____

_____

Notes:

_____

_____

_____

_____

_____

_____

_____

_____

_____

_____

_____

_____

_____

_____

_____

_____

_____

_____

_____

_____

_____

_____

_____

_____

_____

_____

_____

_____

_____

Date: _____

# of days on journey: _____

Journey today from: _____

Journey today to: _____

Departure time: _____

Arrival time: _____

Distance today: _____

Total distance: _____

Nature of country:

_____

_____

_____

_____

Weather:

_____

_____

Temperature: _____   Altitude: _____

Condition of Horses:

_____

_____

_____

_____

_____

_____

_____

Preparation for next day's journey:

_____

_____

_____

_____

Notes:

_____
_____
_____
_____
_____
_____
_____
_____
_____
_____
_____
_____
_____
_____
_____
_____
_____
_____
_____
_____
_____
_____
_____
_____
_____
_____
_____
_____
_____
_____
_____
_____
_____

Date: _____

\# of days on journey: _____

Journey today from: _____

Journey today to: _____

Departure time: _____

Arrival time: _____

Distance today: _____

Total distance: _____

Nature of country:

_____

_____

_____

_____

Weather:

_____

_____

Temperature: _____   Altitude: _____

Condition of Horses:

_____

_____

_____

_____

_____

_____

_____

_____

Preparation for next day's journey:

_____

_____

_____

_____

Notes:

_____

_____

_____

_____

_____

_____

_____

_____

_____

_____

_____

_____

_____

_____

_____

_____

_____

_____

_____

_____

_____

_____

_____

_____

_____

_____

_____

_____

_____

_____

Date: _____

# of days on journey: _____

Journey today from: _____

Journey today to: _____

Departure time: _____

Arrival time: _____

Distance today: _____

Total distance: _____

Nature of country:

_____

_____

_____

_____

Weather:

_____

_____

Temperature: _____   Altitude: _____

Condition of Horses:

_____

_____

_____

_____

_____

_____

_____

_____

Preparation for next day's journey:

_____

_____

_____

_____

Notes:

_____

_____

_____

_____

_____

_____

_____

_____

_____

_____

_____

_____

_____

_____

_____

_____

_____

_____

_____

_____

_____

_____

_____

_____

_____

_____

_____

_____

_____

_____

_____

_____

Date: _____

# of days on journey: _____

Journey today from: _____

Journey today to: _____

Departure time: _____

Arrival time: _____

Distance today: _____

Total distance: _____

Nature of country:

_____

_____

_____

_____

Weather:

_____

_____

Temperature: _____   Altitude: _____

Condition of Horses:

_____

_____

_____

_____

_____

_____

_____

Preparation for next day's journey:

_____

_____

_____

_____

Notes:

Date: _____

# of days on journey: _____

Journey today from: _____

Journey today to: _____

Departure time: _____

Arrival time: _____

Distance today: _____

Total distance: _____

Nature of country:

_____

_____

_____

_____

Weather:

_____

_____

Temperature: _____   Altitude: _____

Condition of Horses:

_____

_____

_____

_____

_____

_____

_____

_____

Preparation for next day's journey:

_____

_____

_____

_____

The Horse Travel Journal

Notes:

_____
_____
_____
_____
_____
_____
_____
_____
_____
_____
_____
_____
_____
_____
_____
_____
_____
_____
_____
_____
_____
_____
_____
_____
_____
_____
_____
_____
_____
_____
_____
_____
_____

Date: _____

# of days on journey: _____

Journey today from: _____

Journey today to: _____

Departure time: _____

Arrival time: _____

Distance today: _____

Total distance: _____

Nature of country:

_____

_____

_____

_____

Weather:

_____

_____

Temperature: _____   Altitude: _____

Condition of Horses:

_____

_____

_____

_____

_____

_____

_____

Preparation for next day's journey:

_____

_____

_____

_____

Notes:

_____

_____

_____

_____

_____

_____

_____

_____

_____

_____

_____

_____

_____

_____

_____

_____

_____

_____

_____

_____

_____

_____

_____

_____

_____

_____

_____

_____

_____

_____

_____

_____

_____

_____

_____

_____

Date: _____

# of days on journey: _____

Journey today from: _____

Journey today to: _____

Departure time: _____

Arrival time: _____

Distance today: _____

Total distance: _____

Nature of country:

_____

_____

_____

_____

Weather:

_____

_____

Temperature: _____   Altitude: _____

Condition of Horses:

_____

_____

_____

_____

_____

_____

_____

Preparation for next day's journey:

_____

_____

_____

_____

Notes:

_____

_____

_____

_____

_____

_____

_____

_____

_____

_____

_____

_____

_____

_____

_____

_____

_____

_____

_____

_____

_____

_____

_____

_____

_____

_____

_____

_____

_____

_____

_____

_____

Date: _____

# of days on journey: _____
Journey today from: _____
Journey today to: _____
Departure time: _____
Arrival time: _____
Distance today: _____
Total distance: _____

Nature of country:

_____
_____
_____
_____

Weather:

_____
_____

Temperature: _____   Altitude: _____

Condition of Horses:

_____
_____
_____
_____
_____
_____
_____

Preparation for next day's journey:

_____
_____
_____
_____

Notes:

_____

_____

_____

_____

_____

_____

_____

_____

_____

_____

_____

_____

_____

_____

_____

_____

_____

_____

_____

_____

_____

_____

_____

_____

_____

_____

_____

_____

_____

Date: _____

# of days on journey: _____

Journey today from: _____

Journey today to: _____

Departure time: _____

Arrival time: _____

Distance today: _____

Total distance: _____

Nature of country:

_____

_____

_____

_____

Weather:

_____

_____

Temperature: _____   Altitude: _____

Condition of Horses:

_____

_____

_____

_____

_____

_____

_____

_____

Preparation for next day's journey:

_____

_____

_____

_____

The Horse Travel Journal

Notes:

_____

_____

_____

_____

_____

_____

_____

_____

_____

_____

_____

_____

_____

_____

_____

_____

_____

_____

_____

_____

_____

_____

_____

_____

_____

_____

_____

_____

_____

Date: _____

# of days on journey: _____

Journey today from: _____

Journey today to: _____

Departure time: _____

Arrival time: _____

Distance today: _____

Total distance: _____

Nature of country:

_____

_____

_____

_____

Weather:

_____

_____

Temperature: _____   Altitude: _____

Condition of Horses:

_____

_____

_____

_____

_____

_____

_____

_____

Preparation for next day's journey:

_____

_____

_____

_____

Notes:

_____

_____

_____

_____

_____

_____

_____

_____

_____

_____

_____

_____

_____

_____

_____

_____

_____

_____

_____

_____

_____

_____

_____

_____

_____

_____

_____

_____

_____

_____

_____

_____

Date: _____

# of days on journey: _____

Journey today from: _____

Journey today to: _____

Departure time: _____

Arrival time: _____

Distance today: _____

Total distance: _____

Nature of country:

_____

_____

_____

_____

Weather:

_____

_____

Temperature: _____   Altitude: _____

Condition of Horses:

_____

_____

_____

_____

_____

_____

_____

_____

Preparation for next day's journey:

_____

_____

_____

_____

Notes:

_____

_____

_____

_____

_____

_____

_____

_____

_____

_____

_____

_____

_____

_____

_____

_____

_____

_____

_____

_____

_____

_____

_____

_____

_____

_____

_____

_____

_____

_____

Date: _____

# of days on journey: _____

Journey today from: _____

Journey today to: _____

Departure time: _____

Arrival time: _____

Distance today: _____

Total distance: _____

Nature of country:

_____

_____

_____

_____

Weather:

_____

_____

Temperature: _____   Altitude: _____

Condition of Horses:

_____

_____

_____

_____

_____

_____

_____

Preparation for next day's journey:

_____

_____

_____

_____

Notes:

_____
_____
_____
_____
_____
_____
_____
_____
_____
_____
_____
_____
_____
_____
_____
_____
_____
_____
_____
_____
_____
_____
_____
_____
_____
_____
_____
_____
_____

Date: _____

# of days on journey: _____

Journey today from: _____

Journey today to: _____

Departure time: _____

Arrival time: _____

Distance today: _____

Total distance: _____

Nature of country:

_____

_____

_____

_____

Weather:

_____

_____

Temperature: _____   Altitude: _____

Condition of Horses:

_____

_____

_____

_____

_____

_____

_____

_____

Preparation for next day's journey:

_____

_____

_____

_____

Notes:

_____

_____

_____

_____

_____

_____

_____

_____

_____

_____

_____

_____

_____

_____

_____

_____

_____

_____

_____

_____

_____

_____

_____

_____

_____

_____

_____

_____

_____

_____

_____

_____

Date: _____

# of days on journey: _____

Journey today from: _____

Journey today to: _____

Departure time: _____

Arrival time: _____

Distance today: _____

Total distance: _____

Nature of country:

_____

_____

_____

_____

Weather:

_____

_____

Temperature: _____   Altitude: _____

Condition of Horses:

_____

_____

_____

_____

_____

_____

_____

_____

Preparation for next day's journey:

_____

_____

_____

_____

Notes:

_____

_____

_____

_____

_____

_____

_____

_____

_____

_____

_____

_____

_____

_____

_____

_____

_____

_____

_____

_____

_____

_____

_____

_____

_____

_____

_____

_____

_____

Date: _____

# of days on journey: _____

Journey today from: _____

Journey today to: _____

Departure time: _____

Arrival time: _____

Distance today: _____

Total distance: _____

Nature of country:

_____
_____
_____
_____

Weather:

_____
_____

Temperature: _____   Altitude: _____

Condition of Horses:

_____
_____
_____
_____
_____
_____
_____
_____

Preparation for next day's journey:

_____
_____
_____
_____

Notes:

_____

_____

_____

_____

_____

_____

_____

_____

_____

_____

_____

_____

_____

_____

_____

_____

_____

_____

_____

_____

_____

_____

_____

_____

_____

_____

_____

_____

_____

_____

Date: _____

# of days on journey: _____

Journey today from: _____

Journey today to: _____

Departure time: _____

Arrival time: _____

Distance today: _____

Total distance: _____

Nature of country:

_____

_____

_____

_____

Weather:

_____

_____

Temperature: _____   Altitude: _____

Condition of Horses:

_____

_____

_____

_____

_____

_____

_____

Preparation for next day's journey:

_____

_____

_____

_____

Notes:

_____

_____

_____

_____

_____

_____

_____

_____

_____

_____

_____

_____

_____

_____

_____

_____

_____

_____

_____

_____

_____

_____

_____

_____

_____

_____

_____

_____

_____

_____

_____

_____

Date: _____

# of days on journey: _____

Journey today from: _____

Journey today to: _____

Departure time: _____

Arrival time: _____

Distance today: _____

Total distance: _____

Nature of country:

_____

_____

_____

_____

Weather:

_____

_____

Temperature: _____   Altitude: _____

Condition of Horses:

_____

_____

_____

_____

_____

_____

_____

Preparation for next day's journey:

_____

_____

_____

_____

Notes:

_____
_____
_____
_____
_____
_____
_____
_____
_____
_____
_____
_____
_____
_____
_____
_____
_____
_____
_____
_____
_____
_____
_____
_____
_____
_____
_____
_____

Date: _____

# of days on journey: _____

Journey today from: _____

Journey today to: _____

Departure time: _____

Arrival time: _____

Distance today: _____

Total distance: _____

Nature of country:

_____

_____

_____

_____

Weather:

_____

_____

Temperature: _____   Altitude: _____

Condition of Horses:

_____

_____

_____

_____

_____

_____

_____

Preparation for next day's journey:

_____

_____

_____

_____

The Horse Travel Journal

Notes:

_____

_____

_____

_____

_____

_____

_____

_____

_____

_____

_____

_____

_____

_____

_____

_____

_____

_____

_____

_____

_____

_____

_____

_____

_____

_____

_____

_____

_____

_____

_____

_____

_____

_____

_____

Date: _____

\# of days on journey: _____

Journey today from: _____

Journey today to: _____

Departure time: _____

Arrival time: _____

Distance today: _____

Total distance: _____

Nature of country:

_____

_____

_____

_____

Weather:

_____

_____

Temperature: _____   Altitude: _____

Condition of Horses:

_____

_____

_____

_____

_____

_____

_____

_____

Preparation for next day's journey:

_____

_____

_____

_____

Notes:

_____

_____

_____

_____

_____

_____

_____

_____

_____

_____

_____

_____

_____

_____

_____

_____

_____

_____

_____

_____

_____

_____

_____

_____

_____

_____

_____

_____

_____

_____

Date: _____

# of days on journey: _____

Journey today from: _____

Journey today to: _____

Departure time: _____

Arrival time: _____

Distance today: _____

Total distance: _____

Nature of country:

_____

_____

_____

_____

Weather:

_____

_____

Temperature: _____   Altitude: _____

Condition of Horses:

_____

_____

_____

_____

_____

_____

_____

Preparation for next day's journey:

_____

_____

_____

_____

Notes:

_____
_____
_____
_____
_____
_____
_____
_____
_____
_____
_____
_____
_____
_____
_____
_____
_____
_____
_____
_____
_____
_____
_____
_____
_____
_____
_____
_____
_____
_____
_____
_____
_____

Date: _____

# of days on journey: _____

Journey today from: _____

Journey today to: _____

Departure time: _____

Arrival time: _____

Distance today: _____

Total distance: _____

Nature of country:

_____

_____

_____

_____

Weather:

_____

_____

Temperature: _____   Altitude: _____

Condition of Horses:

_____

_____

_____

_____

_____

_____

_____

_____

Preparation for next day's journey:

_____

_____

_____

_____

Notes:

_____

_____

_____

_____

_____

_____

_____

_____

_____

_____

_____

_____

_____

_____

_____

_____

_____

_____

_____

_____

_____

_____

_____

_____

_____

_____

_____

_____

_____

_____

_____

_____

Date: _____

# of days on journey: _____

Journey today from: _____

Journey today to: _____

Departure time: _____

Arrival time: _____

Distance today: _____

Total distance: _____

Nature of country:

_____

_____

_____

_____

Weather:

_____

_____

Temperature: _____   Altitude: _____

Condition of Horses:

_____

_____

_____

_____

_____

_____

_____

Preparation for next day's journey:

_____

_____

_____

_____

Notes:

_____
_____
_____
_____
_____
_____
_____
_____
_____
_____
_____
_____
_____
_____
_____
_____
_____
_____
_____
_____
_____
_____
_____
_____
_____
_____
_____
_____
_____
_____
_____
_____
_____
_____
_____

Date: _____

# of days on journey: _____

Journey today from: _____

Journey today to: _____

Departure time: _____

Arrival time: _____

Distance today: _____

Total distance: _____

Nature of country:

_____

_____

_____

_____

Weather:

_____

_____

Temperature: _____   Altitude: _____

Condition of Horses:

_____

_____

_____

_____

_____

_____

_____

_____

Preparation for next day's journey:

_____

_____

_____

_____

Notes:

_____
_____
_____
_____
_____
_____
_____
_____
_____
_____
_____
_____
_____
_____
_____
_____
_____
_____
_____
_____
_____
_____
_____
_____
_____
_____
_____
_____
_____
_____
_____

Date: _____

# of days on journey: _____

Journey today from: _____

Journey today to: _____

Departure time: _____

Arrival time: _____

Distance today: _____

Total distance: _____

Nature of country:

_____

_____

_____

_____

Weather:

_____

_____

Temperature: _____   Altitude: _____

Condition of Horses:

_____

_____

_____

_____

_____

_____

_____

Preparation for next day's journey:

_____

_____

_____

_____

Notes:

Date: _____

\# of days on journey: _____

Journey today from: _____

Journey today to: _____

Departure time: _____

Arrival time: _____

Distance today: _____

Total distance: _____

Nature of country:

_____
_____
_____
_____

Weather:

_____
_____

Temperature: _____   Altitude: _____

Condition of Horses:

_____
_____
_____
_____
_____
_____
_____
_____

Preparation for next day's journey:

_____
_____
_____
_____

The Horse Travel Journal

Notes:

_____

_____

_____

_____

_____

_____

_____

_____

_____

_____

_____

_____

_____

_____

_____

_____

_____

_____

_____

_____

_____

_____

_____

_____

_____

_____

_____

_____

Date: _____

# of days on journey: _____

Journey today from: _____

Journey today to: _____

Departure time: _____

Arrival time: _____

Distance today: _____

Total distance: _____

Nature of country:

_____

_____

_____

_____

Weather:

_____

_____

Temperature: _____   Altitude: _____

Condition of Horses:

_____

_____

_____

_____

_____

_____

_____

Preparation for next day's journey:

_____

_____

_____

_____

The Horse Travel Journal

Notes:

_____
_____
_____
_____
_____
_____
_____
_____
_____
_____
_____
_____
_____
_____
_____
_____
_____
_____
_____
_____
_____
_____
_____
_____
_____
_____
_____
_____
_____
_____

Date: _____

\# of days on journey: _____

Journey today from: _____

Journey today to: _____

Departure time: _____

Arrival time: _____

Distance today: _____

Total distance: _____

Nature of country:

_____
_____
_____
_____

Weather:

_____
_____

Temperature: _____   Altitude: _____

Condition of Horses:

_____
_____
_____
_____
_____
_____
_____
_____

Preparation for next day's journey:

_____
_____
_____
_____

Notes:

_____

_____

_____

_____

_____

_____

_____

_____

_____

_____

_____

_____

_____

_____

_____

_____

_____

_____

_____

_____

_____

_____

_____

_____

_____

_____

_____

_____

_____

_____

_____

_____

_____

Date: _____

# of days on journey: _____

Journey today from: _____

Journey today to: _____

Departure time: _____

Arrival time: _____

Distance today: _____

Total distance: _____

Nature of country:

_____

_____

_____

_____

Weather:

_____

_____

Temperature: _____   Altitude: _____

Condition of Horses:

_____

_____

_____

_____

_____

_____

_____

_____

Preparation for next day's journey:

_____

_____

_____

_____

The Horse Travel Journal

Notes:

_____

_____

_____

_____

_____

_____

_____

_____

_____

_____

_____

_____

_____

_____

_____

_____

_____

_____

_____

_____

_____

_____

_____

_____

_____

_____

_____

_____

_____

_____

_____

_____

_____

Date: _____

# of days on journey: _____

Journey today from: _____

Journey today to: _____

Departure time: _____

Arrival time: _____

Distance today: _____

Total distance: _____

Nature of country:

_____

_____

_____

_____

Weather:

_____

_____

Temperature: _____   Altitude: _____

Condition of Horses:

_____

_____

_____

_____

_____

_____

_____

Preparation for next day's journey:

_____

_____

_____

_____

Notes:

_____
_____
_____
_____
_____
_____
_____
_____
_____
_____
_____
_____
_____
_____
_____
_____
_____
_____
_____
_____
_____
_____
_____
_____
_____
_____
_____
_____
_____
_____
_____

Date: _____

# of days on journey: _____

Journey today from: _____

Journey today to: _____

Departure time: _____

Arrival time: _____

Distance today: _____

Total distance: _____

Nature of country:

_____

_____

_____

_____

Weather:

_____

_____

Temperature: _____   Altitude: _____

Condition of Horses:

_____

_____

_____

_____

_____

_____

_____

_____

Preparation for next day's journey:

_____

_____

_____

_____

Notes:

_____
_____
_____
_____
_____
_____
_____
_____
_____
_____
_____
_____
_____
_____
_____
_____
_____
_____
_____
_____
_____
_____
_____
_____
_____
_____
_____
_____
_____
_____

Date: _____

# of days on journey: _____

Journey today from: _____

Journey today to: _____

Departure time: _____

Arrival time: _____

Distance today: _____

Total distance: _____

Nature of country:

_____

_____

_____

_____

Weather:

_____

_____

Temperature: _____   Altitude: _____

Condition of Horses:

_____

_____

_____

_____

_____

_____

_____

Preparation for next day's journey:

_____

_____

_____

_____

Notes:

_____
_____
_____
_____
_____
_____
_____
_____
_____
_____
_____
_____
_____
_____
_____
_____
_____
_____
_____
_____
_____
_____
_____
_____
_____
_____
_____
_____
_____
_____
_____

Date: _____

# of days on journey: _____

Journey today from: _____

Journey today to: _____

Departure time: _____

Arrival time: _____

Distance today: _____

Total distance: _____

Nature of country:

_____

_____

_____

_____

Weather:

_____

_____

Temperature: _____   Altitude: _____

Condition of Horses:

_____

_____

_____

_____

_____

_____

_____

Preparation for next day's journey:

_____

_____

_____

_____

Notes:

_____
_____
_____
_____
_____
_____
_____
_____
_____
_____
_____
_____
_____
_____
_____
_____
_____
_____
_____
_____
_____
_____
_____
_____
_____
_____
_____
_____
_____
_____

Date: _____

# of days on journey: _____

Journey today from: _____

Journey today to: _____

Departure time: _____

Arrival time: _____

Distance today: _____

Total distance: _____

Nature of country:

_____

_____

_____

_____

Weather:

_____

_____

Temperature: _____   Altitude: _____

Condition of Horses:

_____

_____

_____

_____

_____

_____

_____

Preparation for next day's journey:

_____

_____

_____

_____

Notes:

_____
_____
_____
_____
_____
_____
_____
_____
_____
_____
_____
_____
_____
_____
_____
_____
_____
_____
_____
_____
_____
_____
_____
_____
_____
_____
_____
_____
_____
_____
_____
_____
_____

Date: _____

# of days on journey: _____

Journey today from: _____

Journey today to: _____

Departure time: _____

Arrival time: _____

Distance today: _____

Total distance: _____

Nature of country:

_____

_____

_____

_____

Weather:

_____

_____

Temperature: _____   Altitude: _____

Condition of Horses:

_____

_____

_____

_____

_____

_____

_____

_____

Preparation for next day's journey:

_____

_____

_____

_____

Notes:

_____

_____

_____

_____

_____

_____

_____

_____

_____

_____

_____

_____

_____

_____

_____

_____

_____

_____

_____

_____

_____

_____

_____

_____

_____

_____

_____

_____

_____

Date: _____

# of days on journey: _____

Journey today from: _____

Journey today to: _____

Departure time: _____

Arrival time: _____

Distance today: _____

Total distance: _____

Nature of country:

_____

_____

_____

_____

Weather:

_____

_____

Temperature: _____   Altitude: _____

Condition of Horses:

_____

_____

_____

_____

_____

_____

_____

Preparation for next day's journey:

_____

_____

_____

_____

The Horse Travel Journal

Notes:

_____
_____
_____
_____
_____
_____
_____
_____
_____
_____
_____
_____
_____
_____
_____
_____
_____
_____
_____
_____
_____
_____
_____
_____
_____
_____
_____
_____
_____
_____
_____

Date: _____

# of days on journey: _____

Journey today from: _____

Journey today to: _____

Departure time: _____

Arrival time: _____

Distance today: _____

Total distance: _____

Nature of country:

_____

_____

_____

_____

Weather:

_____

_____

Temperature: _____   Altitude: _____

Condition of Horses:

_____

_____

_____

_____

_____

_____

_____

_____

Preparation for next day's journey:

_____

_____

_____

_____

Notes:

_____
_____
_____
_____
_____
_____
_____
_____
_____
_____
_____
_____
_____
_____
_____
_____
_____
_____
_____
_____
_____
_____
_____
_____
_____
_____
_____
_____
_____

Date: _____

\# of days on journey: _____

Journey today from: _____

Journey today to: _____

Departure time: _____

Arrival time: _____

Distance today: _____

Total distance: _____

Nature of country:

_____

_____

_____

_____

Weather:

_____

_____

Temperature: _____   Altitude: _____

Condition of Horses:

_____

_____

_____

_____

_____

_____

_____

_____

Preparation for next day's journey:

_____

_____

_____

_____

Notes:

_____
_____
_____
_____
_____
_____
_____
_____
_____
_____
_____
_____
_____
_____
_____
_____
_____
_____
_____
_____
_____
_____
_____
_____
_____
_____
_____
_____
_____
_____

Date: _____

# of days on journey: _____

Journey today from: _____

Journey today to: _____

Departure time: _____

Arrival time: _____

Distance today: _____

Total distance: _____

Nature of country:

_____

_____

_____

_____

Weather:

_____

_____

Temperature: _____   Altitude: _____

Condition of Horses:

_____

_____

_____

_____

_____

_____

_____

_____

Preparation for next day's journey:

_____

_____

_____

_____

Notes:

_____

_____

_____

_____

_____

_____

_____

_____

_____

_____

_____

_____

_____

_____

_____

_____

_____

_____

_____

_____

_____

_____

_____

_____

_____

_____

_____

_____

_____

_____

_____

_____

_____

_____

Date: _____

# of days on journey: _____

Journey today from: _____

Journey today to: _____

Departure time: _____

Arrival time: _____

Distance today: _____

Total distance: _____

Nature of country:

_____

_____

_____

_____

Weather:

_____

_____

Temperature: _____   Altitude: _____

Condition of Horses:

_____

_____

_____

_____

_____

_____

_____

Preparation for next day's journey:

_____

_____

_____

_____

Notes:

_____

_____

_____

_____

_____

_____

_____

_____

_____

_____

_____

_____

_____

_____

_____

_____

_____

_____

_____

_____

_____

_____

_____

_____

_____

_____

_____

_____

_____

_____

_____

Date: _____

# of days on journey: _____

Journey today from: _____

Journey today to: _____

Departure time: _____

Arrival time: _____

Distance today: _____

Total distance: _____

Nature of country:

_____

_____

_____

_____

Weather:

_____

_____

Temperature: _____   Altitude: _____

Condition of Horses:

_____

_____

_____

_____

_____

_____

_____

Preparation for next day's journey:

_____

_____

_____

_____

Notes:

_____

_____

_____

_____

_____

_____

_____

_____

_____

_____

_____

_____

_____

_____

_____

_____

_____

_____

_____

_____

_____

_____

_____

_____

_____

_____

_____

_____

_____

_____

_____

_____

_____

Date: _____

# of days on journey: _____

Journey today from: _____

Journey today to: _____

Departure time: _____

Arrival time: _____

Distance today: _____

Total distance: _____

Nature of country:

_____

_____

_____

_____

Weather:

_____

_____

Temperature: _____   Altitude: _____

Condition of Horses:

_____

_____

_____

_____

_____

_____

_____

Preparation for next day's journey:

_____

_____

_____

_____

Notes:

_____
_____
_____
_____
_____
_____
_____
_____
_____
_____
_____
_____
_____
_____
_____
_____
_____
_____
_____
_____
_____
_____
_____
_____
_____
_____
_____
_____
_____
_____
_____
_____
_____
_____

Date: _____

# of days on journey: _____

Journey today from: _____

Journey today to: _____

Departure time: _____

Arrival time: _____

Distance today: _____

Total distance: _____

Nature of country:

_____

_____

_____

_____

Weather:

_____

_____

Temperature: _____   Altitude: _____

Condition of Horses:

_____

_____

_____

_____

_____

_____

_____

Preparation for next day's journey:

_____

_____

_____

_____

Notes:

_____
_____
_____
_____
_____
_____
_____
_____
_____
_____
_____
_____
_____
_____
_____
_____
_____
_____
_____
_____
_____
_____
_____
_____
_____
_____
_____
_____
_____
_____

Date: _____

# of days on journey: _____

Journey today from: _____

Journey today to: _____

Departure time: _____

Arrival time: _____

Distance today: _____

Total distance: _____

Nature of country:

_____

_____

_____

_____

Weather:

_____

_____

Temperature: _____   Altitude: _____

Condition of Horses:

_____

_____

_____

_____

_____

_____

_____

Preparation for next day's journey:

_____

_____

_____

_____

Notes:

_____
_____
_____
_____
_____
_____
_____
_____
_____
_____
_____
_____
_____
_____
_____
_____
_____
_____
_____
_____
_____
_____
_____
_____
_____
_____
_____
_____
_____
_____
_____
_____
_____

Date: _____

\# of days on journey: _____

Journey today from: _____

Journey today to: _____

Departure time: _____

Arrival time: _____

Distance today: _____

Total distance: _____

Nature of country:

_____

_____

_____

_____

Weather:

_____

_____

Temperature: _____   Altitude: _____

Condition of Horses:

_____

_____

_____

_____

_____

_____

_____

Preparation for next day's journey:

_____

_____

_____

_____

Notes:

_____
_____
_____
_____
_____
_____
_____
_____
_____
_____
_____
_____
_____
_____
_____
_____
_____
_____
_____
_____
_____
_____
_____
_____
_____
_____
_____
_____
_____

Date: _____

# of days on journey: _____

Journey today from: _____

Journey today to: _____

Departure time: _____

Arrival time: _____

Distance today: _____

Total distance: _____

Nature of country:

_____

_____

_____

_____

Weather:

_____

_____

Temperature: _____   Altitude: _____

Condition of Horses:

_____

_____

_____

_____

_____

_____

_____

Preparation for next day's journey:

_____

_____

_____

_____

Notes:

_____

_____

_____

_____

_____

_____

_____

_____

_____

_____

_____

_____

_____

_____

_____

_____

_____

_____

_____

_____

_____

_____

_____

_____

_____

_____

_____

_____

_____

_____

_____

_____

Date: _____

# of days on journey: _____

Journey today from: _____

Journey today to: _____

Departure time: _____

Arrival time: _____

Distance today: _____

Total distance: _____

Nature of country:

_____

_____

_____

_____

Weather:

_____

_____

Temperature: _____   Altitude: _____

Condition of Horses:

_____

_____

_____

_____

_____

_____

_____

Preparation for next day's journey:

_____

_____

_____

_____

Notes:

_____

_____

_____

_____

_____

_____

_____

_____

_____

_____

_____

_____

_____

_____

_____

_____

_____

_____

_____

_____

_____

_____

_____

_____

_____

_____

_____

_____

_____

_____

_____

_____

Date: _____

\# of days on journey: _____

Journey today from: _____

Journey today to: _____

Departure time: _____

Arrival time: _____

Distance today: _____

Total distance: _____

Nature of country:

_____

_____

_____

_____

Weather:

_____

_____

Temperature: _____   Altitude: _____

Condition of Horses:

_____

_____

_____

_____

_____

_____

_____

Preparation for next day's journey:

_____

_____

_____

_____

Notes:

_____
_____
_____
_____
_____
_____
_____
_____
_____
_____
_____
_____
_____
_____
_____
_____
_____
_____
_____
_____
_____
_____
_____
_____
_____
_____
_____
_____
_____
_____

Date: _____

# of days on journey: _____

Journey today from: _____

Journey today to: _____

Departure time: _____

Arrival time: _____

Distance today: _____

Total distance: _____

Nature of country:

_____

_____

_____

_____

Weather:

_____

_____

Temperature: _____   Altitude: _____

Condition of Horses:

_____

_____

_____

_____

_____

_____

_____

Preparation for next day's journey:

_____

_____

_____

_____

Notes:

_____

_____

_____

_____

_____

_____

_____

_____

_____

_____

_____

_____

_____

_____

_____

_____

_____

_____

_____

_____

_____

_____

_____

_____

_____

_____

_____

_____

_____

Date: _____

\# of days on journey: _____

Journey today from: _____

Journey today to: _____

Departure time: _____

Arrival time: _____

Distance today: _____

Total distance: _____

Nature of country:

_____

_____

_____

_____

Weather:

_____

_____

Temperature: _____   Altitude: _____

Condition of Horses:

_____

_____

_____

_____

_____

_____

_____

Preparation for next day's journey:

_____

_____

_____

_____

Notes:

_____

_____

_____

_____

_____

_____

_____

_____

_____

_____

_____

_____

_____

_____

_____

_____

_____

_____

_____

_____

_____

_____

_____

_____

_____

_____

_____

_____

_____

_____

_____

_____

The Horse Travel Journal 151

Date: _____

\# of days on journey: _____

Journey today from: _____

Journey today to: _____

Departure time: _____

Arrival time: _____

Distance today: _____

Total distance: _____

Nature of country:

_____
_____
_____
_____

Weather:

_____
_____

Temperature: _____   Altitude: _____

Condition of Horses:

_____
_____
_____
_____
_____
_____
_____

Preparation for next day's journey:

_____
_____
_____
_____

Notes:

_____

_____

_____

_____

_____

_____

_____

_____

_____

_____

_____

_____

_____

_____

_____

_____

_____

_____

_____

_____

_____

_____

_____

_____

_____

_____

_____

_____

Date: _____

# of days on journey: _____

Journey today from: _____

Journey today to: _____

Departure time: _____

Arrival time: _____

Distance today: _____

Total distance: _____

Nature of country:

_____

_____

_____

_____

Weather:

_____

_____

Temperature: _____   Altitude: _____

Condition of Horses:

_____

_____

_____

_____

_____

_____

_____

_____

Preparation for next day's journey:

_____

_____

_____

_____

Notes:

_____

_____

_____

_____

_____

_____

_____

_____

_____

_____

_____

_____

_____

_____

_____

_____

_____

_____

_____

_____

_____

_____

_____

_____

_____

_____

_____

_____

_____

_____

Date: _____

# of days on journey: _____

Journey today from: _____

Journey today to: _____

Departure time: _____

Arrival time: _____

Distance today: _____

Total distance: _____

Nature of country:

_____

_____

_____

_____

Weather:

_____

_____

Temperature: _____   Altitude: _____

Condition of Horses:

_____

_____

_____

_____

_____

_____

_____

_____

Preparation for next day's journey:

_____

_____

_____

_____

Notes:

_____

_____

_____

_____

_____

_____

_____

_____

_____

_____

_____

_____

_____

_____

_____

_____

_____

_____

_____

_____

_____

_____

_____

_____

_____

_____

_____

_____

_____

_____

_____

Date: _____

# of days on journey: _____

Journey today from: _____

Journey today to: _____

Departure time: _____

Arrival time: _____

Distance today: _____

Total distance: _____

Nature of country:

_____

_____

_____

_____

Weather:

_____

_____

Temperature: _____   Altitude: _____

Condition of Horses:

_____

_____

_____

_____

_____

_____

_____

Preparation for next day's journey:

_____

_____

_____

_____

Notes:

_____
_____
_____
_____
_____
_____
_____
_____
_____
_____
_____
_____
_____
_____
_____
_____
_____
_____
_____
_____
_____
_____
_____
_____
_____
_____

Date: _____

# of days on journey: _____

Journey today from: _____

Journey today to: _____

Departure time: _____

Arrival time: _____

Distance today: _____

Total distance: _____

Nature of country:

_____

_____

_____

_____

Weather:

_____

_____

Temperature: _____   Altitude: _____

Condition of Horses:

_____

_____

_____

_____

_____

_____

_____

Preparation for next day's journey:

_____

_____

_____

_____

The Horse Travel Journal

Notes:

_____
_____
_____
_____
_____
_____
_____
_____
_____
_____
_____
_____
_____
_____
_____
_____
_____
_____
_____
_____
_____
_____
_____
_____
_____
_____
_____
_____
_____
_____
_____
_____
_____
_____
_____
_____

Date: _____

\# of days on journey: _____

Journey today from: _____

Journey today to: _____

Departure time: _____

Arrival time: _____

Distance today: _____

Total distance: _____

Nature of country:

_____

_____

_____

_____

Weather:

_____

_____

Temperature: _____   Altitude: _____

Condition of Horses:

_____

_____

_____

_____

_____

_____

_____

_____

Preparation for next day's journey:

_____

_____

_____

_____

The Horse Travel Journal

Notes:

_____

_____

_____

_____

_____

_____

_____

_____

_____

_____

_____

_____

_____

_____

_____

_____

_____

_____

_____

_____

_____

_____

_____

_____

_____

_____

_____

_____

_____

_____

_____

Date: _____

# of days on journey: _____

Journey today from: _____

Journey today to: _____

Departure time: _____

Arrival time: _____

Distance today: _____

Total distance: _____

Nature of country:

_____

_____

_____

_____

Weather:

_____

_____

Temperature: _____   Altitude: _____

Condition of Horses:

_____

_____

_____

_____

_____

_____

_____

Preparation for next day's journey:

_____

_____

_____

_____

Notes:

_____

_____

_____

_____

_____

_____

_____

_____

_____

_____

_____

_____

_____

_____

_____

_____

_____

_____

_____

_____

_____

_____

_____

_____

_____

_____

_____

_____

_____

Date: _____

# of days on journey: _____

Journey today from: _____

Journey today to: _____

Departure time: _____

Arrival time: _____

Distance today: _____

Total distance: _____

Nature of country:

_____

_____

_____

_____

Weather:

_____

_____

Temperature: _____   Altitude: _____

Condition of Horses:

_____

_____

_____

_____

_____

_____

_____

_____

Preparation for next day's journey:

_____

_____

_____

_____

Notes:

_____
_____
_____
_____
_____
_____
_____
_____
_____
_____
_____
_____
_____
_____
_____
_____
_____
_____
_____
_____
_____
_____
_____
_____
_____
_____
_____
_____
_____
_____
_____
_____

Date: _____

# of days on journey: _____

Journey today from: _____

Journey today to: _____

Departure time: _____

Arrival time: _____

Distance today: _____

Total distance: _____

Nature of country:

_____

_____

_____

_____

Weather:

_____

_____

Temperature: _____   Altitude: _____

Condition of Horses:

_____

_____

_____

_____

_____

_____

_____

Preparation for next day's journey:

_____

_____

_____

_____

Notes:

_____
_____
_____
_____
_____
_____
_____
_____
_____
_____
_____
_____
_____
_____
_____
_____
_____
_____
_____
_____
_____
_____
_____
_____
_____
_____
_____
_____
_____

Date: _____

# of days on journey: _____

Journey today from: _____

Journey today to: _____

Departure time: _____

Arrival time: _____

Distance today: _____

Total distance: _____

Nature of country:

_____
_____
_____
_____

Weather:

_____
_____

Temperature: _____   Altitude: _____

Condition of Horses:

_____
_____
_____
_____
_____
_____
_____
_____

Preparation for next day's journey:

_____
_____
_____
_____

Notes:

_____

_____

_____

_____

_____

_____

_____

_____

_____

_____

_____

_____

_____

_____

_____

_____

_____

_____

_____

_____

_____

_____

_____

_____

_____

_____

_____

_____

_____

Date: _____

# of days on journey: _____

Journey today from: _____

Journey today to: _____

Departure time: _____

Arrival time: _____

Distance today: _____

Total distance: _____

Nature of country:

_____

_____

_____

_____

Weather:

_____

_____

Temperature: _____   Altitude: _____

Condition of Horses:

_____

_____

_____

_____

_____

_____

_____

_____

Preparation for next day's journey:

_____

_____

_____

_____

Notes:

_____

_____

_____

_____

_____

_____

_____

_____

_____

_____

_____

_____

_____

_____

_____

_____

_____

_____

_____

_____

_____

_____

_____

_____

_____

_____

_____

_____

_____

_____

Date: _____

# of days on journey: _____

Journey today from: _____

Journey today to: _____

Departure time: _____

Arrival time: _____

Distance today: _____

Total distance: _____

Nature of country:

_____

_____

_____

_____

Weather:

_____

_____

Temperature: _____   Altitude: _____

Condition of Horses:

_____

_____

_____

_____

_____

_____

_____

_____

Preparation for next day's journey:

_____

_____

_____

_____

Notes:

_____

_____

_____

_____

_____

_____

_____

_____

_____

_____

_____

_____

_____

_____

_____

_____

_____

_____

_____

_____

_____

_____

_____

_____

_____

_____

_____

_____

_____

Date: _____

# of days on journey: _____

Journey today from: _____

Journey today to: _____

Departure time: _____

Arrival time: _____

Distance today: _____

Total distance: _____

Nature of country:

_____

_____

_____

_____

Weather:

_____

_____

Temperature: _____   Altitude: _____

Condition of Horses:

_____

_____

_____

_____

_____

_____

_____

_____

Preparation for next day's journey:

_____

_____

_____

_____

Notes:

_____

_____

_____

_____

_____

_____

_____

_____

_____

_____

_____

_____

_____

_____

_____

_____

_____

_____

_____

_____

_____

_____

_____

_____

_____

_____

_____

_____

_____

_____

Date: _____

# of days on journey: _____

Journey today from: _____

Journey today to: _____

Departure time: _____

Arrival time: _____

Distance today: _____

Total distance: _____

Nature of country:

_____

_____

_____

_____

Weather:

_____

_____

Temperature: _____   Altitude: _____

Condition of Horses:

_____

_____

_____

_____

_____

_____

_____

Preparation for next day's journey:

_____

_____

_____

_____

Notes:

_____
_____
_____
_____
_____
_____
_____
_____
_____
_____
_____
_____
_____
_____
_____
_____
_____
_____
_____
_____
_____
_____
_____
_____
_____
_____
_____
_____
_____
_____

Date: _____

# of days on journey: _____

Journey today from: _____

Journey today to: _____

Departure time: _____

Arrival time: _____

Distance today: _____

Total distance: _____

Nature of country:

_____

_____

_____

_____

Weather:

_____

_____

Temperature: _____   Altitude: _____

Condition of Horses:

_____

_____

_____

_____

_____

_____

_____

Preparation for next day's journey:

_____

_____

_____

_____

The Horse Travel Journal

Notes:

_____
_____
_____
_____
_____
_____
_____
_____
_____
_____
_____
_____
_____
_____
_____
_____
_____
_____
_____
_____
_____
_____
_____
_____
_____
_____
_____
_____
_____

Date: _____

# of days on journey: _____

Journey today from: _____

Journey today to: _____

Departure time: _____

Arrival time: _____

Distance today: _____

Total distance: _____

Nature of country:

_____

_____

_____

_____

Weather:

_____

_____

Temperature: _____   Altitude: _____

Condition of Horses:

_____

_____

_____

_____

_____

_____

_____

_____

Preparation for next day's journey:

_____

_____

_____

_____

Notes:

_____

_____

_____

_____

_____

_____

_____

_____

_____

_____

_____

_____

_____

_____

_____

_____

_____

_____

_____

_____

_____

_____

_____

_____

_____

_____

_____

_____

_____

_____

_____

_____

_____

Date: _____

\# of days on journey: _____

Journey today from: _____

Journey today to: _____

Departure time: _____

Arrival time: _____

Distance today: _____

Total distance: _____

Nature of country:

_____

_____

_____

_____

Weather:

_____

_____

Temperature: _____   Altitude: _____

Condition of Horses:

_____

_____

_____

_____

_____

_____

_____

_____

Preparation for next day's journey:

_____

_____

_____

_____

Notes:

_____
_____
_____
_____
_____
_____
_____
_____
_____
_____
_____
_____
_____
_____
_____
_____
_____
_____
_____
_____
_____
_____
_____
_____
_____
_____
_____
_____
_____
_____

Date: _____

# of days on journey: _____

Journey today from: _____

Journey today to: _____

Departure time: _____

Arrival time: _____

Distance today: _____

Total distance: _____

Nature of country:

_____

_____

_____

_____

Weather:

_____

_____

Temperature: _____   Altitude: _____

Condition of Horses:

_____

_____

_____

_____

_____

_____

_____

_____

Preparation for next day's journey:

_____

_____

_____

_____

Notes:

_____
_____
_____
_____
_____
_____
_____
_____
_____
_____
_____
_____
_____
_____
_____
_____
_____
_____
_____
_____
_____
_____
_____
_____
_____
_____
_____
_____
_____

Date: _____

# of days on journey: _____

Journey today from: _____

Journey today to: _____

Departure time: _____

Arrival time: _____

Distance today: _____

Total distance: _____

Nature of country:

_____

_____

_____

_____

Weather:

_____

_____

Temperature: _____   Altitude: _____

Condition of Horses:

_____

_____

_____

_____

_____

_____

_____

_____

Preparation for next day's journey:

_____

_____

_____

_____

Notes:

_____

_____

_____

_____

_____

_____

_____

_____

_____

_____

_____

_____

_____

_____

_____

_____

_____

_____

_____

_____

_____

_____

_____

_____

_____

_____

_____

_____

Date: _____

# of days on journey: _____

Journey today from: _____

Journey today to: _____

Departure time: _____

Arrival time: _____

Distance today: _____

Total distance: _____

Nature of country:

_____
_____
_____
_____

Weather:

_____
_____

Temperature: _____   Altitude: _____

Condition of Horses:

_____
_____
_____
_____
_____
_____
_____
_____

Preparation for next day's journey:

_____
_____
_____
_____

Notes:

_____

_____

_____

_____

_____

_____

_____

_____

_____

_____

_____

_____

_____

_____

_____

_____

_____

_____

_____

_____

_____

_____

_____

_____

_____

_____

_____

_____

_____

Date: _____

\# of days on journey: _____

Journey today from: _____

Journey today to: _____

Departure time: _____

Arrival time: _____

Distance today: _____

Total distance: _____

Nature of country:

_____

_____

_____

_____

Weather:

_____

_____

Temperature: _____   Altitude: _____

Condition of Horses:

_____

_____

_____

_____

_____

_____

_____

_____

Preparation for next day's journey:

_____

_____

_____

_____

Notes:

_____
_____
_____
_____
_____
_____
_____
_____
_____
_____
_____
_____
_____
_____
_____
_____
_____
_____
_____
_____
_____
_____
_____
_____
_____
_____
_____
_____
_____
_____

Date: _____

\# of days on journey: _____

Journey today from: _____

Journey today to: _____

Departure time: _____

Arrival time: _____

Distance today: _____

Total distance: _____

Nature of country:

_____

_____

_____

_____

Weather:

_____

_____

Temperature: _____   Altitude: _____

Condition of Horses:

_____

_____

_____

_____

_____

_____

_____

_____

Preparation for next day's journey:

_____

_____

_____

_____

Notes:

_____

_____

_____

_____

_____

_____

_____

_____

_____

_____

_____

_____

_____

_____

_____

_____

_____

_____

_____

_____

_____

_____

_____

_____

_____

_____

Date: _____

# of days on journey: _____

Journey today from: _____

Journey today to: _____

Departure time: _____

Arrival time: _____

Distance today: _____

Total distance: _____

Nature of country:

_____

_____

_____

_____

Weather:

_____

_____

Temperature: _____   Altitude: _____

Condition of Horses:

_____

_____

_____

_____

_____

_____

_____

_____

Preparation for next day's journey:

_____

_____

_____

_____

The Horse Travel Journal

Notes:

_____

_____

_____

_____

_____

_____

_____

_____

_____

_____

_____

_____

_____

_____

_____

_____

_____

_____

_____

_____

_____

_____

_____

_____

_____

_____

_____

_____

_____

_____

_____

Date: _____

# of days on journey: _____

Journey today from: _____

Journey today to: _____

Departure time: _____

Arrival time: _____

Distance today: _____

Total distance: _____

Nature of country:

_____
_____
_____
_____

Weather:

_____
_____

Temperature: _____   Altitude: _____

Condition of Horses:

_____
_____
_____
_____
_____
_____
_____
_____

Preparation for next day's journey:

_____
_____
_____
_____

Notes:

_____
_____
_____
_____
_____
_____
_____
_____
_____
_____
_____
_____
_____
_____
_____
_____
_____
_____
_____
_____
_____
_____
_____
_____
_____
_____
_____
_____
_____
_____
_____
_____

Date: _____

# of days on journey: _____

Journey today from: _____

Journey today to: _____

Departure time: _____

Arrival time: _____

Distance today: _____

Total distance: _____

Nature of country:

_____
_____
_____
_____

Weather:

_____
_____

Temperature: _____   Altitude: _____

Condition of Horses:

_____
_____
_____
_____
_____
_____
_____

Preparation for next day's journey:

_____
_____
_____
_____

Notes:

_____
_____
_____
_____
_____
_____
_____
_____
_____
_____
_____
_____
_____
_____
_____
_____
_____
_____
_____
_____
_____
_____
_____
_____
_____
_____
_____
_____
_____

Date: _____

# of days on journey: _____

Journey today from: _____

Journey today to: _____

Departure time: _____

Arrival time: _____

Distance today: _____

Total distance: _____

Nature of country:

_____

_____

_____

_____

Weather:

_____

_____

Temperature: _____   Altitude: _____

Condition of Horses:

_____

_____

_____

_____

_____

_____

_____

_____

Preparation for next day's journey:

_____

_____

_____

_____

Notes:

_____
_____
_____
_____
_____
_____
_____
_____
_____
_____
_____
_____
_____
_____
_____
_____
_____
_____
_____
_____
_____
_____
_____
_____
_____
_____
_____
_____
_____
_____
_____
_____

Date: _____

# of days on journey: _____

Journey today from: _____

Journey today to: _____

Departure time: _____

Arrival time: _____

Distance today: _____

Total distance: _____

Nature of country:

_____

_____

_____

_____

Weather:

_____

_____

Temperature: _____   Altitude: _____

Condition of Horses:

_____

_____

_____

_____

_____

_____

_____

_____

Preparation for next day's journey:

_____

_____

_____

_____

Notes:

_____

_____

_____

_____

_____

_____

_____

_____

_____

_____

_____

_____

_____

_____

_____

_____

_____

_____

_____

_____

_____

_____

_____

_____

_____

_____

_____

_____

_____

_____

Date: _____

# of days on journey: _____

Journey today from: _____

Journey today to: _____

Departure time: _____

Arrival time: _____

Distance today: _____

Total distance: _____

Nature of country:

_____

_____

_____

_____

Weather:

_____

_____

Temperature: _____   Altitude: _____

Condition of Horses:

_____

_____

_____

_____

_____

_____

_____

_____

Preparation for next day's journey:

_____

_____

_____

_____

The Horse Travel Journal

Notes:

_____
_____
_____
_____
_____
_____
_____
_____
_____
_____
_____
_____
_____
_____
_____
_____
_____
_____
_____
_____
_____
_____
_____
_____
_____
_____
_____
_____
_____
_____
_____
_____
_____
_____
_____

Date: _____

# of days on journey: _____

Journey today from: _____

Journey today to: _____

Departure time: _____

Arrival time: _____

Distance today: _____

Total distance: _____

Nature of country:

_____

_____

_____

_____

Weather:

_____

_____

Temperature: _____   Altitude: _____

Condition of Horses:

_____

_____

_____

_____

_____

_____

_____

_____

Preparation for next day's journey:

_____

_____

_____

_____

The Horse Travel Journal

Notes:

_____

_____

_____

_____

_____

_____

_____

_____

_____

_____

_____

_____

_____

_____

_____

_____

_____

_____

_____

_____

_____

_____

_____

_____

_____

_____

_____

_____

_____

Date: _____

\# of days on journey: _____

Journey today from: _____

Journey today to: _____

Departure time: _____

Arrival time: _____

Distance today: _____

Total distance: _____

Nature of country:

_____

_____

_____

_____

Weather:

_____

_____

Temperature: _____   Altitude: _____

Condition of Horses:

_____

_____

_____

_____

_____

_____

_____

_____

Preparation for next day's journey:

_____

_____

_____

_____

Notes:

_____
_____
_____
_____
_____
_____
_____
_____
_____
_____
_____
_____
_____
_____
_____
_____
_____
_____
_____
_____
_____
_____
_____
_____
_____
_____
_____
_____
_____
_____
_____
_____

Date: _____

# of days on journey: _____

Journey today from: _____

Journey today to: _____

Departure time: _____

Arrival time: _____

Distance today: _____

Total distance: _____

Nature of country:

_____

_____

_____

_____

Weather:

_____

_____

Temperature: _____   Altitude: _____

Condition of Horses:

_____

_____

_____

_____

_____

_____

_____

_____

Preparation for next day's journey:

_____

_____

_____

_____

The Horse Travel Journal

Notes:

_____
_____
_____
_____
_____
_____
_____
_____
_____
_____
_____
_____
_____
_____
_____
_____
_____
_____
_____
_____
_____
_____
_____
_____
_____
_____
_____
_____
_____

Date: _____

# of days on journey: _____

Journey today from: _____

Journey today to: _____

Departure time: _____

Arrival time: _____

Distance today: _____

Total distance: _____

Nature of country:

_____

_____

_____

_____

Weather:

_____

_____

Temperature: _____   Altitude: _____

Condition of Horses:

_____

_____

_____

_____

_____

_____

_____

_____

Preparation for next day's journey:

_____

_____

_____

_____

Notes:

_____
_____
_____
_____
_____
_____
_____
_____
_____
_____
_____
_____
_____
_____
_____
_____
_____
_____
_____
_____
_____
_____
_____
_____
_____
_____
_____
_____
_____
_____
_____

Date: _____

# of days on journey: _____

Journey today from: _____

Journey today to: _____

Departure time: _____

Arrival time: _____

Distance today: _____

Total distance: _____

Nature of country:

_____

_____

_____

_____

Weather:

_____

_____

Temperature: _____   Altitude: _____

Condition of Horses:

_____

_____

_____

_____

_____

_____

_____

_____

Preparation for next day's journey:

_____

_____

_____

_____

Notes:

Date: _____

# of days on journey: _____

Journey today from: _____

Journey today to: _____

Departure time: _____

Arrival time: _____

Distance today: _____

Total distance: _____

Nature of country:

_____

_____

_____

_____

Weather:

_____

_____

Temperature: _____   Altitude: _____

Condition of Horses:

_____

_____

_____

_____

_____

_____

_____

_____

Preparation for next day's journey:

_____

_____

_____

_____

Notes:

_____
_____
_____
_____
_____
_____
_____
_____
_____
_____
_____
_____
_____
_____
_____
_____
_____
_____
_____
_____
_____
_____
_____
_____
_____
_____
_____
_____
_____
_____
_____

Date: _____

# of days on journey: _____

Journey today from: _____

Journey today to: _____

Departure time: _____

Arrival time: _____

Distance today: _____

Total distance: _____

Nature of country:

_____

_____

_____

_____

Weather:

_____

_____

Temperature: _____   Altitude: _____

Condition of Horses:

_____

_____

_____

_____

_____

_____

_____

_____

Preparation for next day's journey:

_____

_____

_____

_____

Notes:

_____

_____

_____

_____

_____

_____

_____

_____

_____

_____

_____

_____

_____

_____

_____

_____

_____

_____

_____

_____

_____

_____

_____

_____

_____

_____

_____

_____

_____

Date: _____

# of days on journey: _____

Journey today from: _____

Journey today to: _____

Departure time: _____

Arrival time: _____

Distance today: _____

Total distance: _____

Nature of country:

_____

_____

_____

_____

Weather:

_____

_____

Temperature: _____   Altitude: _____

Condition of Horses:

_____

_____

_____

_____

_____

_____

_____

_____

Preparation for next day's journey:

_____

_____

_____

_____

Notes:

_____
_____
_____
_____
_____
_____
_____
_____
_____
_____
_____
_____
_____
_____
_____
_____
_____
_____
_____
_____
_____
_____
_____
_____
_____
_____
_____
_____
_____
_____
_____

Date: _____

# of days on journey: _____

Journey today from: _____

Journey today to: _____

Departure time: _____

Arrival time: _____

Distance today: _____

Total distance: _____

Nature of country:

_____

_____

_____

_____

Weather:

_____

_____

Temperature: _____   Altitude: _____

Condition of Horses:

_____

_____

_____

_____

_____

_____

_____

_____

Preparation for next day's journey:

_____

_____

_____

_____

Notes:

_____

_____

_____

_____

_____

_____

_____

_____

_____

_____

_____

_____

_____

_____

_____

_____

_____

_____

_____

_____

_____

_____

_____

_____

_____

_____

_____

_____

_____

_____

Date: _____

# of days on journey: _____

Journey today from: _____

Journey today to: _____

Departure time: _____

Arrival time: _____

Distance today: _____

Total distance: _____

Nature of country:

_____

_____

_____

_____

Weather:

_____

_____

Temperature: _____   Altitude: _____

Condition of Horses:

_____

_____

_____

_____

_____

_____

_____

Preparation for next day's journey:

_____

_____

_____

_____

Notes:

Date: _____

# of days on journey: _____

Journey today from: _____

Journey today to: _____

Departure time: _____

Arrival time: _____

Distance today: _____

Total distance: _____

Nature of country:

_____

_____

_____

_____

Weather:

_____

_____

Temperature: _____   Altitude: _____

Condition of Horses:

_____

_____

_____

_____

_____

_____

_____

_____

Preparation for next day's journey:

_____

_____

_____

_____

Notes:

_____

_____

_____

_____

_____

_____

_____

_____

_____

_____

_____

_____

_____

_____

_____

_____

_____

_____

_____

_____

_____

_____

_____

_____

_____

_____

_____

_____

_____

Date: _____

# of days on journey: _____

Journey today from: _____

Journey today to: _____

Departure time: _____

Arrival time: _____

Distance today: _____

Total distance: _____

Nature of country:

_____
_____
_____
_____

Weather:

_____
_____

Temperature: _____   Altitude: _____

Condition of Horses:

_____
_____
_____
_____
_____
_____
_____
_____

Preparation for next day's journey:

_____
_____
_____
_____

Notes:

_____

_____

_____

_____

_____

_____

_____

_____

_____

_____

_____

_____

_____

_____

_____

_____

_____

_____

_____

_____

_____

_____

_____

_____

_____

_____

_____

_____

Date: _____

# of days on journey: _____

Journey today from: _____

Journey today to: _____

Departure time: _____

Arrival time: _____

Distance today: _____

Total distance: _____

Nature of country:

_____

_____

_____

_____

Weather:

_____

_____

Temperature: _____   Altitude: _____

Condition of Horses:

_____

_____

_____

_____

_____

_____

_____

Preparation for next day's journey:

_____

_____

_____

_____

Notes:

_____
_____
_____
_____
_____
_____
_____
_____
_____
_____
_____
_____
_____
_____
_____
_____
_____
_____
_____
_____
_____
_____
_____
_____
_____
_____
_____
_____
_____

Date: _____

# of days on journey: _____

Journey today from: _____

Journey today to: _____

Departure time: _____

Arrival time: _____

Distance today: _____

Total distance: _____

Nature of country:

_____

_____

_____

_____

Weather:

_____

_____

Temperature: _____   Altitude: _____

Condition of Horses:

_____

_____

_____

_____

_____

_____

_____

Preparation for next day's journey:

_____

_____

_____

_____

Notes:

_____

_____

_____

_____

_____

_____

_____

_____

_____

_____

_____

_____

_____

_____

_____

_____

_____

_____

_____

_____

_____

_____

_____

_____

_____

_____

_____

_____

_____

Date: _____

# of days on journey: _____

Journey today from: _____

Journey today to: _____

Departure time: _____

Arrival time: _____

Distance today: _____

Total distance: _____

Nature of country:

_____

_____

_____

_____

Weather:

_____

_____

Temperature: _____   Altitude: _____

Condition of Horses:

_____

_____

_____

_____

_____

_____

_____

_____

Preparation for next day's journey:

_____

_____

_____

_____

Notes:

_____

_____

_____

_____

_____

_____

_____

_____

_____

_____

_____

_____

_____

_____

_____

_____

_____

_____

_____

_____

_____

_____

_____

_____

_____

_____

_____

_____

Date: _____

# of days on journey: _____

Journey today from: _____

Journey today to: _____

Departure time: _____

Arrival time: _____

Distance today: _____

Total distance: _____

Nature of country:

_____

_____

_____

_____

Weather:

_____

_____

Temperature: _____   Altitude: _____

Condition of Horses:

_____

_____

_____

_____

_____

_____

_____

_____

Preparation for next day's journey:

_____

_____

_____

_____

Notes:

_____

_____

_____

_____

_____

_____

_____

_____

_____

_____

_____

_____

_____

_____

_____

_____

_____

_____

_____

_____

_____

_____

_____

_____

_____

_____

_____

_____

_____

Date: _____

# of days on journey: _____

Journey today from: _____

Journey today to: _____

Departure time: _____

Arrival time: _____

Distance today: _____

Total distance: _____

Nature of country:

_____

_____

_____

_____

Weather:

_____

_____

Temperature: _____   Altitude: _____

Condition of Horses:

_____

_____

_____

_____

_____

_____

_____

_____

Preparation for next day's journey:

_____

_____

_____

_____

Notes:

_____

_____

_____

_____

_____

_____

_____

_____

_____

_____

_____

_____

_____

_____

_____

_____

_____

_____

_____

_____

_____

_____

_____

_____

_____

_____

_____

_____

Date: _____

# of days on journey: _____

Journey today from: _____

Journey today to: _____

Departure time: _____

Arrival time: _____

Distance today: _____

Total distance: _____

Nature of country:

_____

_____

_____

_____

Weather:

_____

_____

Temperature: _____   Altitude: _____

Condition of Horses:

_____

_____

_____

_____

_____

_____

_____

Preparation for next day's journey:

_____

_____

_____

_____

Notes:

_____
_____
_____
_____
_____
_____
_____
_____
_____
_____
_____
_____
_____
_____
_____
_____
_____
_____
_____
_____
_____
_____
_____
_____
_____
_____
_____
_____
_____

Date: _____

# of days on journey: _____

Journey today from: _____

Journey today to: _____

Departure time: _____

Arrival time: _____

Distance today: _____

Total distance: _____

Nature of country:

_____

_____

_____

_____

Weather:

_____

_____

Temperature: _____   Altitude: _____

Condition of Horses:

_____

_____

_____

_____

_____

_____

_____

_____

Preparation for next day's journey:

_____

_____

_____

_____

Notes:

_____

_____

_____

_____

_____

_____

_____

_____

_____

_____

_____

_____

_____

_____

_____

_____

_____

_____

_____

_____

_____

_____

_____

_____

_____

_____

_____

_____

_____

_____

_____

_____

Date: _____

# of days on journey: _____

Journey today from: _____

Journey today to: _____

Departure time: _____

Arrival time: _____

Distance today: _____

Total distance: _____

Nature of country:

_____

_____

_____

_____

Weather:

_____

_____

Temperature: _____   Altitude: _____

Condition of Horses:

_____

_____

_____

_____

_____

_____

_____

Preparation for next day's journey:

_____

_____

_____

_____

The Horse Travel Journal

Notes:

_____
_____
_____
_____
_____
_____
_____
_____
_____
_____
_____
_____
_____
_____
_____
_____
_____
_____
_____
_____
_____
_____
_____
_____
_____
_____
_____
_____
_____
_____
_____
_____

Date: _____

# of days on journey: _____

Journey today from: _____

Journey today to: _____

Departure time: _____

Arrival time: _____

Distance today: _____

Total distance: _____

Nature of country:

_____

_____

_____

_____

Weather:

_____

_____

Temperature: _____   Altitude: _____

Condition of Horses:

_____

_____

_____

_____

_____

_____

_____

Preparation for next day's journey:

_____

_____

_____

_____

Notes:

_____
_____
_____
_____
_____
_____
_____
_____
_____
_____
_____
_____
_____
_____
_____
_____
_____
_____
_____
_____
_____
_____
_____
_____
_____
_____
_____
_____
_____

Date: _____

# of days on journey: _____

Journey today from: _____

Journey today to: _____

Departure time: _____

Arrival time: _____

Distance today: _____

Total distance: _____

Nature of country:

_____

_____

_____

_____

Weather:

_____

_____

Temperature: _____   Altitude: _____

Condition of Horses:

_____

_____

_____

_____

_____

_____

_____

_____

Preparation for next day's journey:

_____

_____

_____

_____

The Horse Travel Journal

Notes:

_____

_____

_____

_____

_____

_____

_____

_____

_____

_____

_____

_____

_____

_____

_____

_____

_____

_____

_____

_____

_____

_____

_____

_____

_____

_____

_____

_____

_____

_____

_____

_____

Date: _____

\# of days on journey: _____

Journey today from: _____

Journey today to: _____

Departure time: _____

Arrival time: _____

Distance today: _____

Total distance: _____

Nature of country:

_____

_____

_____

_____

Weather:

_____

_____

Temperature: _____   Altitude: _____

Condition of Horses:

_____

_____

_____

_____

_____

_____

_____

_____

Preparation for next day's journey:

_____

_____

_____

_____

Notes:

_____
_____
_____
_____
_____
_____
_____
_____
_____
_____
_____
_____
_____
_____
_____
_____
_____
_____
_____
_____
_____
_____
_____
_____
_____
_____
_____
_____
_____
_____
_____
_____

Date: _____

# of days on journey: _____

Journey today from: _____

Journey today to: _____

Departure time: _____

Arrival time: _____

Distance today: _____

Total distance: _____

Nature of country:

_____

_____

_____

_____

Weather:

_____

_____

Temperature: _____   Altitude: _____

Condition of Horses:

_____

_____

_____

_____

_____

_____

_____

Preparation for next day's journey:

_____

_____

_____

_____

Notes:

_____
_____
_____
_____
_____
_____
_____
_____
_____
_____
_____
_____
_____
_____
_____
_____
_____
_____
_____
_____
_____
_____
_____
_____
_____
_____
_____
_____

Date: _____

# of days on journey: _____

Journey today from: _____

Journey today to: _____

Departure time: _____

Arrival time: _____

Distance today: _____

Total distance: _____

Nature of country:

_____

_____

_____

_____

Weather:

_____

_____

Temperature: _____   Altitude: _____

Condition of Horses:

_____

_____

_____

_____

_____

_____

_____

_____

Preparation for next day's journey:

_____

_____

_____

_____

Notes:

_____

_____

_____

_____

_____

_____

_____

_____

_____

_____

_____

_____

_____

_____

_____

_____

_____

_____

_____

_____

_____

_____

_____

_____

_____

_____

_____

_____

Date: _____

# of days on journey: _____

Journey today from: _____

Journey today to: _____

Departure time: _____

Arrival time: _____

Distance today: _____

Total distance: _____

Nature of country:

_____

_____

_____

_____

Weather:

_____

_____

Temperature: _____   Altitude: _____

Condition of Horses:

_____

_____

_____

_____

_____

_____

_____

Preparation for next day's journey:

_____

_____

_____

_____

Notes:

_____
_____
_____
_____
_____
_____
_____
_____
_____
_____
_____
_____
_____
_____
_____
_____
_____
_____
_____
_____
_____
_____
_____
_____
_____
_____
_____
_____
_____
_____
_____
_____
_____

Date: _____

\# of days on journey: _____

Journey today from: _____

Journey today to: _____

Departure time: _____

Arrival time: _____

Distance today: _____

Total distance: _____

Nature of country:

_____

_____

_____

_____

Weather:

_____

_____

Temperature: _____   Altitude: _____

Condition of Horses:

_____

_____

_____

_____

_____

_____

_____

Preparation for next day's journey:

_____

_____

_____

_____

Notes:

_____

_____

_____

_____

_____

_____

_____

_____

_____

_____

_____

_____

_____

_____

_____

_____

_____

_____

_____

_____

_____

_____

_____

_____

_____

_____

_____

_____

_____

_____

_____

_____

_____

_____

_____

_____

Date: _____

\# of days on journey: _____

Journey today from: _____

Journey today to: _____

Departure time: _____

Arrival time: _____

Distance today: _____

Total distance: _____

Nature of country:

_____

_____

_____

_____

Weather:

_____

_____

Temperature: _____   Altitude: _____

Condition of Horses:

_____

_____

_____

_____

_____

_____

_____

Preparation for next day's journey:

_____

_____

_____

_____

Notes:

_____
_____
_____
_____
_____
_____
_____
_____
_____
_____
_____
_____
_____
_____
_____
_____
_____
_____
_____
_____
_____
_____
_____
_____
_____
_____
_____
_____
_____
_____

Date: _____

# of days on journey: _____

Journey today from: _____

Journey today to: _____

Departure time: _____

Arrival time: _____

Distance today: _____

Total distance: _____

Nature of country:

_____

_____

_____

_____

Weather:

_____

_____

Temperature: _____   Altitude: _____

Condition of Horses:

_____

_____

_____

_____

_____

_____

_____

_____

Preparation for next day's journey:

_____

_____

_____

_____

Notes:

_____
_____
_____
_____
_____
_____
_____
_____
_____
_____
_____
_____
_____
_____
_____
_____
_____
_____
_____
_____
_____
_____
_____
_____
_____
_____
_____
_____
_____

Date: _____

# of days on journey: _____

Journey today from: _____

Journey today to: _____

Departure time: _____

Arrival time: _____

Distance today: _____

Total distance: _____

Nature of country:

_____

_____

_____

_____

Weather:

_____

_____

Temperature: _____   Altitude: _____

Condition of Horses:

_____

_____

_____

_____

_____

_____

_____

_____

Preparation for next day's journey:

_____

_____

_____

_____

The Horse Travel Journal

Notes:

_____
_____
_____
_____
_____
_____
_____
_____
_____
_____
_____
_____
_____
_____
_____
_____
_____
_____
_____
_____
_____
_____
_____
_____
_____
_____
_____
_____

Date: _____

# of days on journey: _____

Journey today from: _____

Journey today to: _____

Departure time: _____

Arrival time: _____

Distance today: _____

Total distance: _____

Nature of country:

_____

_____

_____

_____

Weather:

_____

_____

Temperature: _____   Altitude: _____

Condition of Horses:

_____

_____

_____

_____

_____

_____

_____

_____

Preparation for next day's journey:

_____

_____

_____

_____

Notes:

_____

_____

_____

_____

_____

_____

_____

_____

_____

_____

_____

_____

_____

_____

_____

_____

_____

_____

_____

_____

_____

_____

_____

_____

_____

_____

_____

_____

Date: _____

# of days on journey: _____

Journey today from: _____

Journey today to: _____

Departure time: _____

Arrival time: _____

Distance today: _____

Total distance: _____

Nature of country:

_____

_____

_____

_____

Weather:

_____

_____

Temperature: _____   Altitude: _____

Condition of Horses:

_____

_____

_____

_____

_____

_____

_____

Preparation for next day's journey:

_____

_____

_____

_____

Notes:

_____
_____
_____
_____
_____
_____
_____
_____
_____
_____
_____
_____
_____
_____
_____
_____
_____
_____
_____
_____
_____
_____
_____
_____
_____
_____
_____
_____
_____
_____

Date: _____

# of days on journey: _____

Journey today from: _____

Journey today to: _____

Departure time: _____

Arrival time: _____

Distance today: _____

Total distance: _____

Nature of country:

_____

_____

_____

_____

Weather:

_____

_____

Temperature: _____   Altitude: _____

Condition of Horses:

_____

_____

_____

_____

_____

_____

_____

_____

Preparation for next day's journey:

_____

_____

_____

_____

Notes:

_____

_____

_____

_____

_____

_____

_____

_____

_____

_____

_____

_____

_____

_____

_____

_____

_____

_____

_____

_____

_____

_____

_____

_____

_____

_____

_____

_____

Date: _____

# of days on journey: _____

Journey today from: _____

Journey today to: _____

Departure time: _____

Arrival time: _____

Distance today: _____

Total distance: _____

Nature of country:

_____

_____

_____

_____

Weather:

_____

_____

Temperature: _____   Altitude: _____

Condition of Horses:

_____

_____

_____

_____

_____

_____

_____

_____

Preparation for next day's journey:

_____

_____

_____

_____

Notes:

_____

_____

_____

_____

_____

_____

_____

_____

_____

_____

_____

_____

_____

_____

_____

_____

_____

_____

_____

_____

_____

_____

_____

_____

_____

_____

_____

_____

_____

_____

Date: _____

# of days on journey: _____

Journey today from: _____

Journey today to: _____

Departure time: _____

Arrival time: _____

Distance today: _____

Total distance: _____

Nature of country:

_____

_____

_____

_____

Weather:

_____

_____

Temperature: _____   Altitude: _____

Condition of Horses:

_____

_____

_____

_____

_____

_____

_____

_____

Preparation for next day's journey:

_____

_____

_____

_____

Notes:

Date: _____

# of days on journey: _____

Journey today from: _____

Journey today to: _____

Departure time: _____

Arrival time: _____

Distance today: _____

Total distance: _____

Nature of country:

_____

_____

_____

_____

Weather:

_____

_____

Temperature: _____   Altitude: _____

Condition of Horses:

_____

_____

_____

_____

_____

_____

_____

Preparation for next day's journey:

_____

_____

_____

_____

Notes:

_____
_____
_____
_____
_____
_____
_____
_____
_____
_____
_____
_____
_____
_____
_____
_____
_____
_____
_____
_____
_____
_____
_____
_____
_____
_____
_____

Date: _____

# of days on journey: _____

Journey today from: _____

Journey today to: _____

Departure time: _____

Arrival time: _____

Distance today: _____

Total distance: _____

Nature of country:

_____

_____

_____

_____

Weather:

_____

_____

Temperature: _____   Altitude: _____

Condition of Horses:

_____

_____

_____

_____

_____

_____

_____

_____

Preparation for next day's journey:

_____

_____

_____

_____

Notes:

_____

_____

_____

_____

_____

_____

_____

_____

_____

_____

_____

_____

_____

_____

_____

_____

_____

_____

_____

_____

_____

_____

_____

_____

_____

_____

_____

_____

_____

_____

_____

_____

Date: _____

\# of days on journey: _____

Journey today from: _____

Journey today to: _____

Departure time: _____

Arrival time: _____

Distance today: _____

Total distance: _____

Nature of country:

_____

_____

_____

_____

Weather:

_____

_____

Temperature: _____   Altitude: _____

Condition of Horses:

_____

_____

_____

_____

_____

_____

_____

_____

Preparation for next day's journey:

_____

_____

_____

_____

Notes:

_____

_____

_____

_____

_____

_____

_____

_____

_____

_____

_____

_____

_____

_____

_____

_____

_____

_____

_____

_____

_____

_____

_____

_____

_____

_____

_____

_____

_____

Date: _____

# of days on journey: _____

Journey today from: _____

Journey today to: _____

Departure time: _____

Arrival time: _____

Distance today: _____

Total distance: _____

Nature of country:

_____

_____

_____

_____

Weather:

_____

_____

Temperature: _____   Altitude: _____

Condition of Horses:

_____

_____

_____

_____

_____

_____

_____

_____

Preparation for next day's journey:

_____

_____

_____

_____

Notes:

Date: _____

# of days on journey: _____

Journey today from: _____

Journey today to: _____

Departure time: _____

Arrival time: _____

Distance today: _____

Total distance: _____

Nature of country:

_____

_____

_____

_____

Weather:

_____

_____

Temperature: _____   Altitude: _____

Condition of Horses:

_____

_____

_____

_____

_____

_____

_____

Preparation for next day's journey:

_____

_____

_____

_____

Notes:

Date: _____

# of days on journey: _____

Journey today from: _____

Journey today to: _____

Departure time: _____

Arrival time: _____

Distance today: _____

Total distance: _____

Nature of country:

_____

_____

_____

_____

Weather:

_____

_____

Temperature: _____   Altitude: _____

Condition of Horses:

_____

_____

_____

_____

_____

_____

_____

Preparation for next day's journey:

_____

_____

_____

_____

Notes:

_____

_____

_____

_____

_____

_____

_____

_____

_____

_____

_____

_____

_____

_____

_____

_____

_____

_____

_____

_____

_____

_____

_____

_____

_____

_____

_____

_____

_____

_____

LONG RIDER PICTIONARY

The images on the following pages are designed to assist Long Riders as they are travel with their horse in foreign countries which present linguistic difficulties.

The Pictionary is not meant to replace a standard phrase-book in a local language. Every equestrian explorer knows that the better he or she communicates the better are their chances of equestrian success. Yet knowing how to greet people, count in the local currency or ask for simple directions is not enough for a Long Rider. Modern nomads know from experience that the words they need, such as oats, hay, stable, farrier, saddle, etc., are not to be found in even the best phrase-books.

That is why the Long Rider Pictionary provides images of those objects and situations most likely to be of use or concern to equestrian explorers. Included are images of light and heavy horses, grain and hay, water and bucket, stable and camp, saddle and pack saddle, horse shoe and farrier, vet and equine body parts, as well as images of dangerous wild animals and difficult terrain such as mountains, deserts, rivers etc.

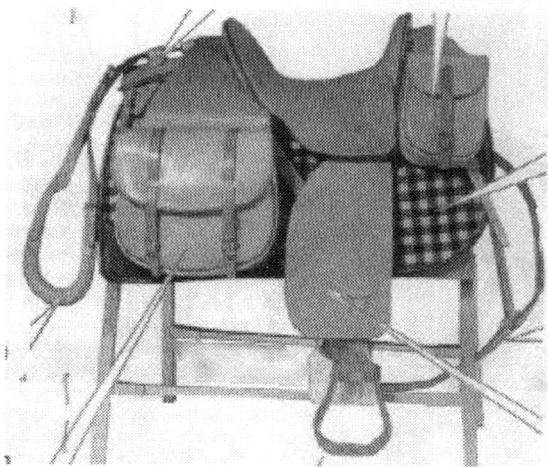

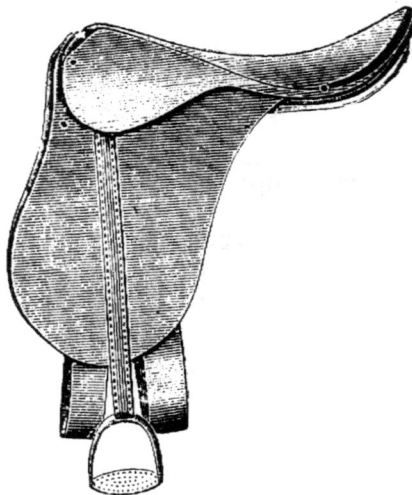

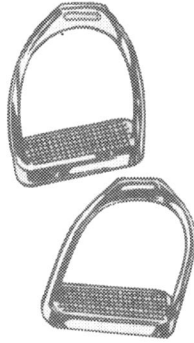

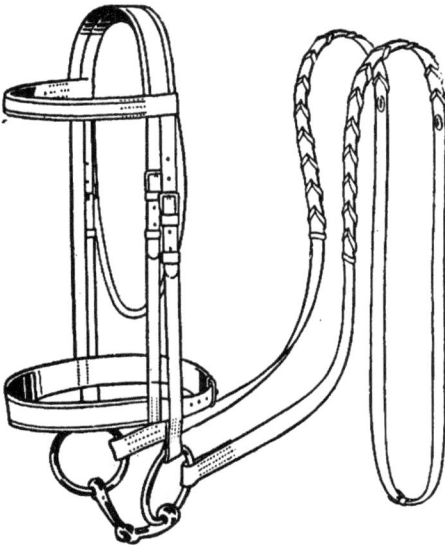

Above: Canadian Long Rider Stan Walchuk with his adjustable pack saddle

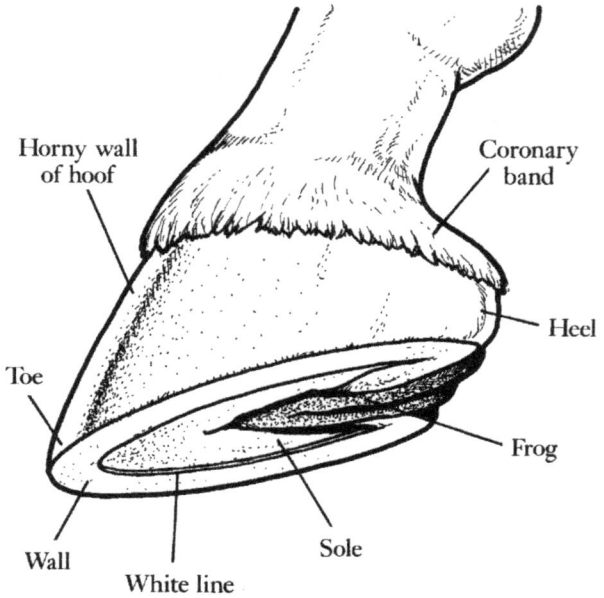

Horny wall
of hoof

Coronary
band

Heel

Toe

Frog

Wall

Sole

White line

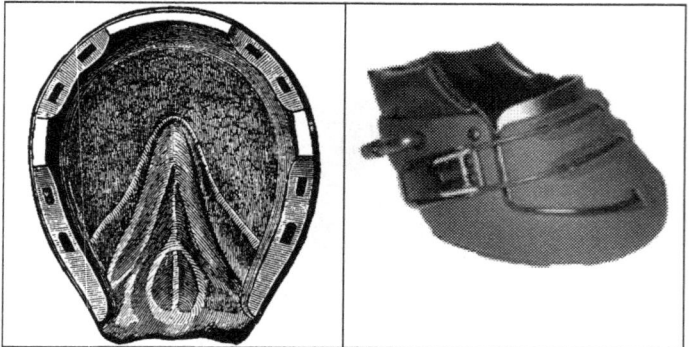

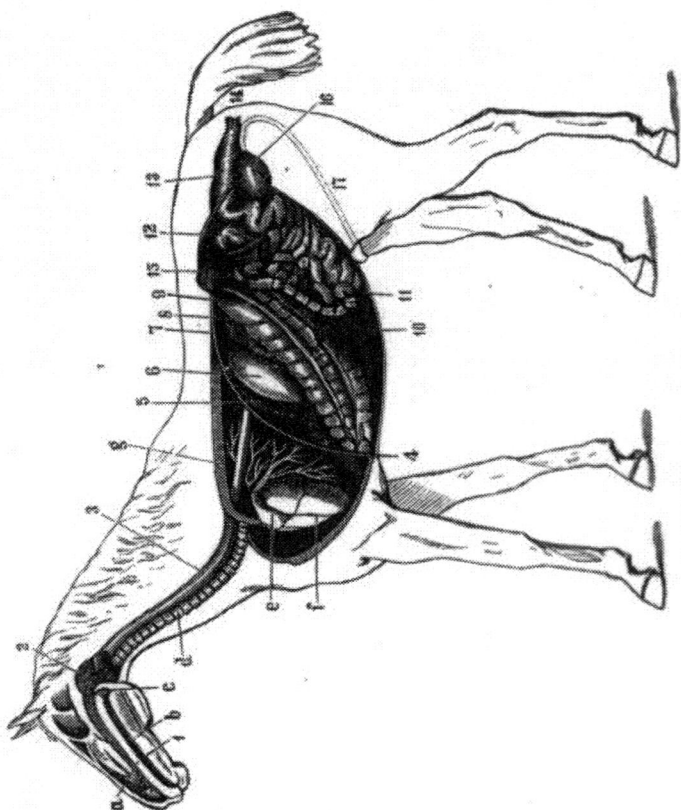

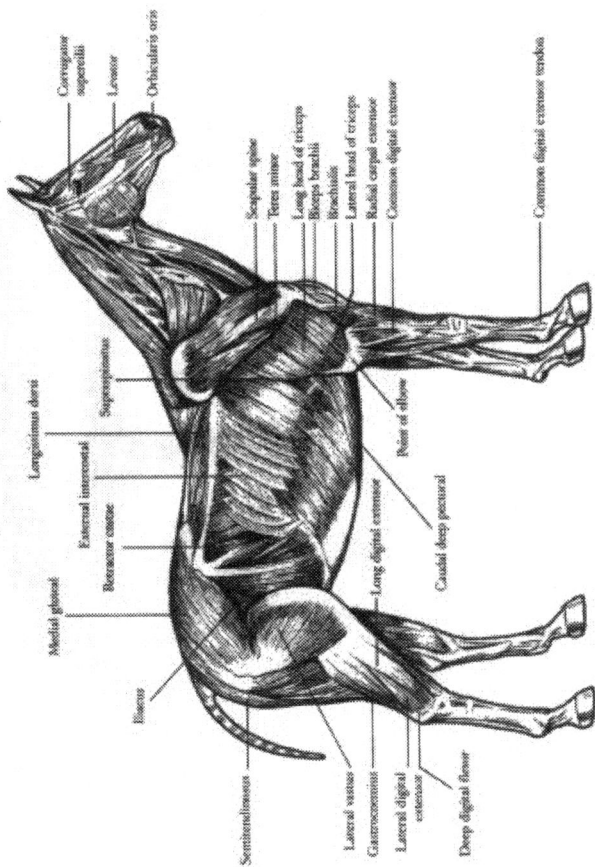

Corrugator supercilii
Levator
Orbicularis oris

Scapular spine
Teres minor
Long head of triceps
Biceps brachii
Brchiis
Lateral head of triceps
Radial carpal extensor
Common digital extensor

Common digital extensor tendon

Latissimus dorsi
Supraspinatus

Lateral intertranse
Retractor coste

Medial gluteal

Biceps

Semitendinosus

Point of elbow

Long digital extensor

Caudal deep pectoral

Lateral vastus
Gastrocnemius
Lateral digital extensor

Deep digital flexor

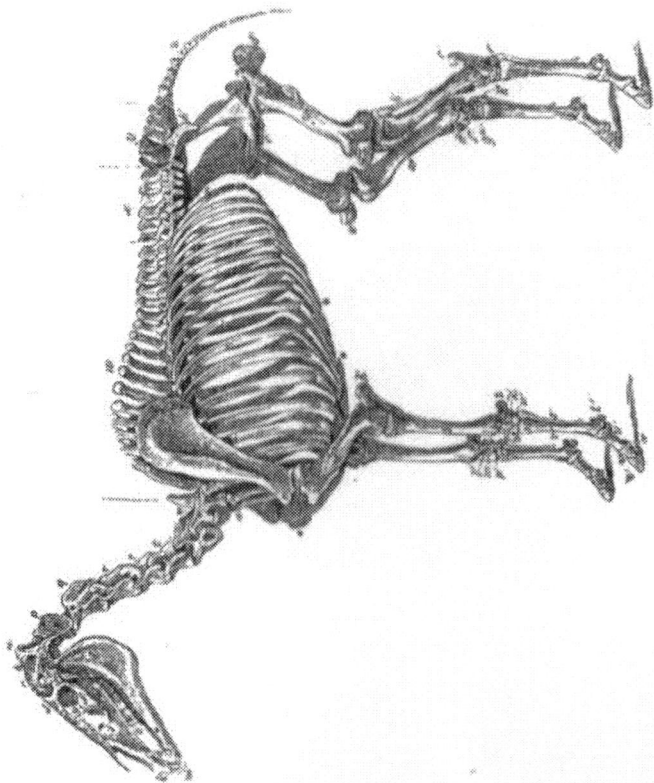

DANGER

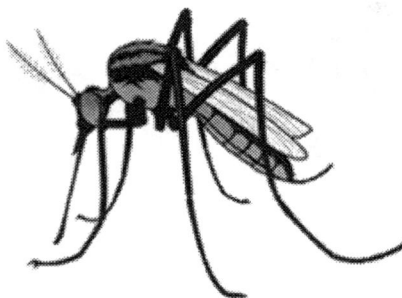